DESTINATION
FLORIDA

Miami Beach, seaside resort to metropolitan Miami.

DESTINATION FLORIDA

Photographs: Udo Bernhart
Text: Ernst Marchel

WINDSOR BOOKS
INTERNATIONAL

California flamingoes in Busch Gardens, the fourth largest zoo in the United States.

CONTENTS

Ernst Marchel

America's Green Thumb	8

Flat as a Billiard Table	8
Orange Blossoms and Sabal Palms	10
A Zoological Wonderland	11
Pascua Florida, 1513	12
The Indians Fight for their Land	15
Railways and Hotels	16
Just One Enormous Amusement Park?	21

Anthology

Swamp, Sand and Sea	22

Reflections and Commentaries
on the Sunshine State

Ernst Marchel

Concise Travel Guide	48

Map	48
General Information	48
Points of Interest	48

List of Sources and Illustrations   56

The Don CeSar, a first class hotel in St. Petersburg Beach.

AMERICA'S GREEN THUMB

Florida – the very name is enough to conjure up all manner of images. Sweet-smelling orchids, palm trees waving in the wind, azure seas, white sandy beaches, lazy days and everlasting sunshine. Like a green thumb pointing downwards, the "Sunshine State" is bathed by the Atlantic on its eastern side and the Gulf of Mexico on its western side. Of all the regions in the United States, Florida is probably the best known among non-Americans. Its attractions, with their extravagant and dynamic publicity campaigns which pull in the visitors, range from a railway completed in 1912 reaching all the way to Key West, to the MGM-Disney Film Studios, opened in May 1989.

Putting Florida into a book is like trying to squeeze ten thousand oranges into a pint jar. Between its northern boundary with Georgia and Key West, the most southerly point of mainland USA, there are so many secrets waiting to be uncovered that just one visit is not enough. The two quite different seaboards, the freshwater Lake Okeechobee, rivers running through jungle landscapes and the unique wilderness of the Everglades – everything has its own flavour and character. Florida's cities, too, vary enormously: pulsating Miami, respectable St. Augustine, mushrooming Orlando.

Getting around in Florida is easy. Fast roads crisscross the state, jets land at modern airports, and the trains try to run on time. And yet, despite all the high technology and the many theme parks, it is still possible to experience the unforgettable delight of strolling along a deserted beach. As they say in Florida, "once you've felt the sand of Florida in your shoes, you'll be sure to come back". There is always a beach nearby: it is never more than about sixty miles/one hundred kilometres from any point in Florida to the nearest beach.

Flat as a Billiard Table

Several hundred million years ago, volcanoes spewed out magma from deep within the earth into the primeval ocean, and so created the base on which were formed present-day Florida and many of the Caribbean islands. Over the next few million years, the mountains made by these volcanoes sank back into the warm waters of the ocean. Layer upon layer of marine sediments settled on top. These enormous strata of lime and sandstone – known as the Florida aquifer – go down to a depth of more than 13,000 feet/4,000 metres. Only there does the bedrock begin.

The land was to remain under water for a long time to come. While the dinosaurs were tramping through swamps throughout the rest of the world, sea was still billowing over Florida. Only recently – about twenty million years ago – did the narrow strip of land which was later to be named Florida emerge from the waves. Thus, compared with other parts of the world, Florida is still in its infancy. Gradually, plants and animals from the north and the tropical south colonised the new land. The ice ages, although they brought no glaciers to Florida, lowered the level of the world's oceans and therefore, exposed new areas of sea bed. The limestone was shaped by the last ice age and many centuries of rain and tides. Gradually, the peninsula began to take on its present form. Constant erosion by waves, wind and rain has made Florida as flat as a billiard table: its highest point is less than four hundred feet/one hundred-fifteen metres above sea level. This nameless high point lies in the north of Florida, near its border with Alabama, where rolling hills make a strong contrast to the flat landscape of the south of the state.

The clear, bubbling mineral springs, of which there are thousands in the northern part of Florida, owe their existence to the porous, water-retaining limestone and sandstone strata which form the bedrock of the peninsula. Non-porous strata of clay lie within the water, held under pressure by the bedrock and the surface and, in places where the clay strata are thinner, the water breaks through to the surface, forming gushing freshwater springs.

Florida is divided by its natural features into several different regions. The wet coastal strip around the

Freshwater pool or the "real" coast? Not only here, south of Clearwater, are both options available side by side. Florida's Gulf coast is renowned for its fine white sand.

The islands of the Florida Keys lie like a string of pearls in the Gulf of Mexico, the extreme southern outposts of Florida and the United States.

Atlantic and Gulf coasts influences the nature of the soil for a distance of some sixty miles/one hundred kilometres inland. These flat regions are densely covered with rich vegetation. Along the coasts there are coral reefs, bays and sand dunes, numerous peninsulas, and hundreds of small offshore islands, many of them uncharted. The southernmost tip of Florida consists of shell limestone and coral cliffs, and east of the Florida Keys are to be found the last living coral reefs of America.

The south of the peninsula, between "Big Water" (the 460 square mile/1,200 square kilometre freshwater Lake Okeechobee) and the Everglades was all originally swampland. In fact, the Everglades are actually made up of a slow-flowing river over fifty miles/eighty-five kilometres wide and only an inch or two deep. It has its source in Lake Okeechobee, 125 miles/200 kilometres further north. Large tracts of the Everglades have been drained to provide land for agriculture and building; today, only about 2,300 square miles/6,000 square kilometres of swampland remain.

The central lakeland region of Florida, from the Okefenokee Swamp in the state of Georgia down to Lake Okeechobee, is covered with a whole network of rivers and lakes, as well as numerous cold springs. The north of Florida – the area around Tallahassee – is a flat plateau where extensive pine forests grow and where there are many small lakes and artesian springs. To the west of Tallahassee lie the Marianna Lowlands. The characteristic features of this region are the sinkholes formed by the collapse of thin strata of shell limestone, and the Marianna limestone caves which lie above the water table. The "Florida Caverns" were created by water slowly eating its way through the limestone strata, and creating stalagmites, calcite columns and other formations, including the so-called "organ pipes".

The lack of resistance of shell limestone to water also shows up in the many rivers of northern Florida, which were formed as a result of the water breaking through to the earth's surface. The rivers betray the history of their origin in the stretches where they run underground, in other words, where the water has been unable to break through to the surface.

Orange Blossoms and Sabal Palms

In Florida, tropical plants bloom harmoniously alongside plants from more northerly regions: its flora unites the best of both worlds. At least 314 different types of

Here the Everglades, a protected area of swampland, sink into the ocean. In actual fact, the Everglades consist of a very slow-flowing river which has its source in Lake Okeechobee, 125 miles/200 kilometres to the north.

trees have been counted, half of them indigenous species. Pine trees are very common, and large forests of them cover most of the north and northwest of Florida. Tulip trees, maples and sweet gums also grow in this part of the state. Florida has the orange blossom as its state flower, and the state tree is the sabal or palmetto palm, which you see wherever you go, reaching majestically for the sky.

In central Florida, the cypress, magnolia, Florida hickory and various species of oak all flourish. In the southern regions tropical trees predominate: the coconut palm and royal palm grow here, as well as the gumbo-limbo, live-oak and West Indian mahogany. The low-growing cabbage palm feels most at home in Florida's coastal areas. Thanks to the clearing process of the timber industry, there now remain only struggling remnants of the ancient forests which once existed.

In the gardens of Florida, each plant has found its own niche. The duckweed, wild iris and rush prefer swamps and shallow water, while the water hyacinth, extremely beautiful but due to its rampant growth not exactly well-loved, can choke entire river basins in no time at all. In the Everglades, epiphytic (air-living) plants perch in the forks of branches in the larger trees, and ferns, lianas and orchids radiate an exotic beauty.

In the Everglades, a difference in altitude of as little as a-foot-and-a-half/one-half metre produces a change in the flora. At altitudes of more than thirteen feet/four metres above sea-level, there are dense pine forests, a little lower grow the hardwood forests (hammocks), followed by the reed and sedge swamps. Cypress swamps are found just six-and-a-half feet/two metres above sea-level, and right down at the water's edge grow the mangroves, which can survive in salt-water.

The soft, rolling countryside of northern Florida is famous for its fantastic show of colours. The azalea, camellia, oleander, hibiscus, gardenia, jasmine, poinsettia, trumpet creeper and morning glory thrive everywhere, and in places where the temperature does not drop below 55 degrees Fahrenheit/15 degrees Celsius, the regal poinciana tree and the lush bougainvillea blossom in their vivid colours.

A Zoological Wonderland

Wherever they went in Florida, the early explorers all reported an incredible diversity of animal species. Only a few decades ago, when the road from Tampa to Miami was being built, there was an enormous range of bird life along the Tamiami Trail. Today, ninety percent of the birds which once lived in the Everglades have disappeared. Nevertheless, in those areas where the natural habitat of the animals is protected, Florida remains a zoological wonderland.

Of the more than eighty species of terrestrial mammals which still live in Florida, the black bear, grey fox, puma, panther and other wild cats are among the rarest. Deer generally graze everywhere, except for the little white-tailed key deer, which is now to be found only in very small numbers on the island of Big Pine Key. There are still large numbers of squirrels, hares, racoons and opossums, but the otter and mink, which for a long time were hunted for their skins, have been almost wiped out. Armadilloes snuffle noisily after insects, and wild hogs are to be found in wooded areas.

Civilisation represents a very serious threat to the manatees which were once common here. Today, they are almost extinct, and the few hundred specimens still living around Florida are strictly protected. In the waters along the western coast, these placid marine mammals graze: every day they consume more than one hundred pounds/forty-five kilograms of sea grass and water hyacinths. In the lakes, rivers and swamps live greenish-black alligators, which have been a protected species for many years now. Fortunately, the soft, supple skin from the underbelly of this reptile is no longer used to make belts, shoes or wallets. The North American crocodile lives a retiring life in remote salt-water reaches of the southern Everglades.

The burning-hot sand serves as an incubator for sea turtles: they bury their eggs in it. The once very numerous loggerhead and leatherback turtles have now also, unfortunately, nearly all disappeared. There remain just a few loggerheads, whose hard, dark-brindled shells with plates arranged like roof shingles used to be made into jewellery and trinkets, living off the islands of Sanibel and Captiva. In the swamps, smaller species of the turtle live in peaceful co-existence with frogs, lizards and other small reptiles. Also to be found in Florida are the rattlesnake, coral snake, water mocassin and red rat-snake.

Ornithologists have recorded and observed more than four hundred species of birds in Florida. In the shallow lakes and swamps, herons and egrets stand as if on stilts, and the long-legged ibis struts around in a deliberate manner. Anhingas, more commonly known as snakebirds, swim and dive for fish, which they spear with their pointed beaks. With a single flick, the fish is hurled into the air, skillfully caught, and swallowed. After every feeding, the anhinga has to make for the bank or the nearest tree and spread out its wings to dry, as it has no water-repellent oils to protect its feathers. On the highway through the Florida Keys, you can admire fish eagle nests, artistically perched on telephone poles. Florida's conservationists are paying particular attention to the spoonbills and storks, whose numbers have already been severely depleted, but which are still to be found in the Everglades. Just like many humans, there are geese and other birds of passage which come to spend the winter in Florida, and they find a safe haven in the nature reserves. Sandpipers, pelicans and gulls in the coastal areas remain undisturbed by the proximity of humans.

The most popular of Florida's mammals, however, is the dolphin; even when in captivity, its great intelligence and friendliness astonishes mankind. Dolphins, which normally live in fairly large schools, will from time to time suddenly appear in a bay or alongside a boat, which they will then usually accompany for quite some time, bringing back memories of the clicking and whistling Flipper, who helped make Florida's coastal waters famous.

Pascua Florida, 1513

Archaeologists believe that the first people to reach Florida, eight thousand years before our reckoning, were hunters (their descendants were later called Indians by the European settlers), and that over the course of the centuries they spread throughout the area. Various tribes grew up, and the people lived in fortressed villages and farmed the land. Corn, gourds, beans and tobacco were grown, while the oceans and rivers provided a wide variety of fish and shellfish, and in the woods red deer were hunted. Remains from those days include arrowheads and other weapons, parts of tools, and earthenware and ceramic shards, which can be seen in such places as the Indian Temple Mound Museum in Fort Walton. In many places there are still temple mounds and burial mounds hidden under the vegetation, some of them more than sixty-five feet/twenty metres high.

When the first Europeans landed on the peninsula, it was inhabited by some 10,000 Indians. The Apalachee hunted in the northwest, the Tumuca lived in the northeast, and the war-like Calusa inhabited and defended the Everglades. Smaller tribes such as the Tequeslas and the Ais lived along southeast coast, or intermingled with the large neighbouring tribes.

The written history of Florida begins in the year 1513, when the Spanish conquistador Juan Ponce de León was the first European to set foot in Florida. Shortly before landing near what is now St. Augustine on the east coast, he celebrated Easter ("Pascua Florida") on board his ship, and he decided to call the land he had discovered Florida. However, the Indians were

Deepsea game fishing is just one of many sports on offer in Florida. It doesn't always have to be anything as grand as the Great White Shark. Here we have a "dolphin", a species of dorado much prized in Florida for its tasty flesh.

Ernest Hemingway's house in Key West is open to the public. The famous author lived here for twelve years from 1928 onwards, and wrote several of his books while a Florida resident.

ready for the fray, and thwarted his plans to find the gold treasures and "fountain of youth" which were supposed to exist. Juan Ponce de León returned to Cuba. Eight years later, on his second expedition in 1521, he landed on the western coast with the intention of founding a colony in the hinterland. Skirmishes with the Indians and a fever among his men decimated their numbers, and after Ponce de León himself was hit by an arrow during a battle, he was obliged to return once again to Cuba, where he died a few weeks later.

Subsequent attempts by the Spaniards to turn Florida into a permanent colony also initially failed. It was not just the embittered resistance of the Indians to the hostile invaders which exhausted them, but also quite simply the country itself. When the troops of Hernando de Soto, who explored the region from Tampa to Tallahassee, and the armies of Tristán de Luna, Vasques de Aylon and Pánfilo de Narváez scoured the land in their search for treasure, all their dreams of conquest and wealth were shattered by interminable swamps, swarms of mosquitoes and hurricanes.

The next attempt was initiated by a Frenchman. In the spring of 1565, René Goulaine de Laudonnière landed with a group of Huguenots – French Protestants – on the northeastern coast of Florida, and founded the settlement of Fort Caroline. The Spaniards, however, were not prepared to let the Huguenots compete with them for Florida; they sent Pedro Menendez de Aviles across the Atlantic, and in the autumn of 1565, with 1,500 soldiers and settlers, he founded St. Augustine, the oldest surviving settlement in North America. Pedro Menendez defeated the French at Fort Caroline, had them all hanged, and renamed the fort San Mateo. Two years later, San Mateo was won back by the French in a bloody battle which cost many lives. The Spanish settlement of St. Augustine was not spared, either: in 1586 it was plundered by Sir Francis Drake, and part of it was burned down. The Spanish, however, were now unstoppable. They built a large number of forts and missions in the north of Florida and converted the Indians, whose numbers had already been severely depleted by European diseases and innumerable battles, to Catholicism.

Since it seemed that Florida was firmly in Spanish hands, the English seafarers and conquerors turned their attention initially to the territories to the north of Florida, and in the seventeenth century founded colonies in Georgia and South Carolina. Using these as bases, they pushed southwards and began to make trouble for the Spanish. Between 1702 and 1706 they

Key West, the jewel of the Keys, is favoured with superb weather and the most magnificent flora. As well as its white villas and orchid-filled gardens, this popular holiday destination also has some cultural gems to visit.

destroyed nearly all the Spanish forts and mission stations, and made slaves of the Indians whom the Spaniards had baptised. The English bid for Florida became stronger and stronger, and there followed more (unsuccessful) attacks. Finally, however, they achieved their goal: in 1763, at the negotiating table in Paris, the Spanish exchanged Florida for Cuba, which the English had conquered shortly before.

For the next few decades, the fate of Florida continued to hang in the balance: with a peace treaty signed in 1783, England ceded Florida back to Spain (this time in exchange for The Bahamas); part of western Florida was given to the French; the British eventually seized Pensacola, and for a short time, Amelia Island even became a Mexican colony. In 1819, Florida underwent its last change of ownership. Spain, whose empire was gradually falling apart, handed Florida over to the United States for five million dollars. In 1821 the treaty was ratified, and in 1845 Florida became the twenty-seventh state in the union.

The Indians Fight for their Land

Once Tallahassee had been declared the capital of Florida in 1823, a wave of white settlers streamed into the land. Unimpressed by the claims of the Seminole Indians to ownership, they ploughed up the land and planted orange groves. By this time the majority of the original inhabitants of Florida had already been wiped out by the Europeans, and now only isolated members of the once proud Indian tribes still lived in the woods and swamps. Creek Indians, driven out of Georgia by the English and forced southwards, took refuge in the Everglades. They soon became known as "Seminoles", which means exiles. The Indians, themselves driven out of their homeland, gave shelter to escaped Negro slaves. This act initiated the First Seminole War. In order to get the slaves back, General Andrew Jackson marched his troops into Florida and launched a fierce attack on the Indians.

In the years that followed, the Seminoles lived peacefully in the seclusion of the Everglades and Tampa Bay and simply had to accept the further advance of the white interlopers. Some minor skirmishes followed, and General Andrew Jackson – who in the meantime had been elected the seventh president of the United States – decided to eradicate the Seminoles once and for all. He had not, however, expected that the Indians would put up such a hard fight for their property. Certainly a few chiefs were forced to surrender, but others, like Chief Osceola, put up a stubborn resistance. By his courage and intelligence Chief Osceola won the respect even of his enemies. For three years, he and his people fought what amounted to a guerilla war, but the Indian leader was finally taken prisoner during fraudulent peace negotiations, and died. After a further seven years of warfare, the loss of 1,500 lives and the deportation of thousands of Indians to Oklahoma, the United States Government was finally able to declare victory in 1842. So ended the Second Seminole War, a bloody war of unsurpassed cruelty.

A few hundred Seminoles escaped deportation and hid in their home territory, the swamps. And, here they were again subjected to surprise attacks by the whites. For a further three years, they resisted the superior forces, until they, too, were taken off to Oklahoma. That was the end of the Third, and last, Seminole War. This time only a handful were able to escape deportation, and they spent the last few decades of the nineteenth century living a nomadic life in the swamps. As in many other parts of the United States, so, too, in Florida the Indians had fought for their homeland. Today, some 1,500 descendants of the Seminoles and 500 Miccosukees live in the Everglades and their inaccessible hinterland; they remain unvanquished, and they still have no peace treaty.

Sixteen years after Florida officially achieved statehood, it was heard announcing its secession from the union. The state administration had decided to back the Confederates. During the Civil War from 1861 to 1865, 16,000 soldiers from Florida fought in the Confederate Army against the northern states. Since fortunately there were no major battles on Florida's soil, the post-war period was not as hard here as it was in other southern states. In northern and central Florida, white settlers and returning soldiers tried to farm the poor soil, which earned them the nickname "crackers", after the cracked corn which was one of the staple foods of these industrious but poor people.

Railways and Hotels

Around 1880, the wheel of history began to turn faster in Florida, and events took place which have left their mark on the land up to the present day. Swamps were systematically drained, huge orange plantations were laid out, Cuban cigar-makers settled in Tampa, and in Tarpon Springs, Greek immigrants began diving for sponges. Many people found their wealth in the first round of real estate speculation, and two immensely rich men set about trying to conquer Florida.

These far-sighted entrepreneurs were Henry B. Plant and Henry M. Flagler. They recognised that the state had tourist potential. Both can rightly be said to have been the creators of modern Florida. At an enormous cost and in the face of huge difficulties, they built railways right across the state. Plant concentrated on the west coast while Flagler opened up the east coast. At the same time as they were building the railways, both also began putting up luxury hotels, to attract sun-starved tourists from Chicago and New York. Flagler opened his first hotel in St. Augustine with great ceremony in 1885. Resolutely, he pushed on southwards with the tracks for his East Coast Railway, heading for Miami. Miami was at that time an unnoticed village consisting of a few wooden shacks, but Henry Flagler was on his way to conquer it. Henry Plant, whose Atlantic Coast Line had reached the town of Tampa, invested in 1889 in the construction of the Tampa Bay Hotel.

As the nineteenth century was drawing to a close, Florida had already earned itself the reputation of being the exclusive playground of the millionaires who were eager to exchange the wintry weather of New England for beach parties and palm trees. In 1904, Henry Flagler decided to continue his railway line right down to Key West. This was to be his most ambitious project ever. Up to then, he had planned his railways only as a means of conveying patrons to the luxury accommodations he had built along the east coast. It took forty bridges and eight years of hard work to link together the islands of the Florida Keys. In 1912 the route was completed: in the northern city of Jacksonville, Flagler was able to board the first train bound for Key West in the extreme south of Florida.

In the years which followed, there was a rapid increase in the population of the state. The first tourists in automobiles arrived, and wealthy elderly Americans chose Florida for their retirement homes. The more prosperous middle class families were also able to afford a holiday on a Florida beach. Property prices rose, estate agents were making money hand over fist. Millions of dollars changed hands.

Then, suddenly, there came a slump for Florida. In 1926, December was cold and rainy, and by Florida's standards the month began rather unpleasantly. Just at that time the directors of the biggest banks in the United States were meeting in St. Petersburg, discussing commercial and land investments. It was raining. The next day it rained even more, and the day after that it poured. The bank directors left, and throughout the country they told of how dreadful the weather was in Florida. When, in the spring of 1927, a cold wave destroyed the citrus harvest, the tourists also packed their suitcases. Hotels and houses stood empty, property prices fell through the floor. As if that were not enough, following a hot humid summer of that

The skyline of downtown Miami: skyscrapers and highways are also part of the Florida scene. But beware: all that glitters is not gold, and many a palm tree is made of plastic.

Homes in these modern developments flanking the Intracoastal Waterway, linking Miami with Fort Lauderdale, remain much sought.

The Port of Miami is one of the ports of call on many Caribbean cruises. Here, The Norway, the longest passenger ship in the world, is just dropping anchor.

disastrous year, Florida was devastated by a hurricane. Two years later, most of the investors were ruined in the stock market crash, leaving the "Sunshine State" in shreds. It was not until well into the 1930s that Florida recovered from its climatic catastrophes and the recession.

In 1935 there was another hurricane, which devastated many of the Caribbean islands and swept across the Florida Keys. Flagler's railway line was destroyed, but its bridges were subsequently used in the construction of the new US Highway 1. The days of the great iron horse were over, the "Havana Special" would never again steam down to Key West.

Once the consequences of the stock market crash and the latest natural disaster had been overcome, Florida became, in the late 1940s and early 1950s, a symbol of progress and the future of the United States. The most important technical innovation in the 1950s was the building of the NASA Space Center at Cape Canaveral. After the shock of Sputnik and frustration over the fact that first man in space was not American but Russian, the Kennedy administration forced through the expansion of the space programme. So it was that on 20 July 1969 American time (in Europe it was already 21 July), two Americans set foot on the Earth's satellite: astronauts Neil Armstrong and Edwin Aldrin were the first men to leave their footprints on the moon.

Space travel experts and scientists, computer firms and armaments manufacturers settled on the east coast around Orlando. Enormous sums of money circulated, and deals involving millions of dollars were transacted via the subsidiaries of international banks. People from every corner of America came flooding into Florida to find work, and immigrants also tried their luck in a new home. For everyone, the mild, sunny climate was an added attraction.

Ever larger, ever more luxurious villas were built, magnificent hotels sprang up, and tourism grew into the most important sector of Florida's economy. Places like Palm Beach and Miami Beach are now among the most popular resorts in the United States. The booming economy brought in its wake hundreds of thousands of tourists eager for travel, and the exodus of senior citizens from the northern states began. This time, Florida was conquered by people who wanted to spend their last years in its golden climate.

During the turbulent 1960s, there were considerable tensions in Florida, as elsewhere. In many of the large cities there were bloody confrontations between

Exclusive yacht clubs and hotels on Turnberry Isle, one of the little islands along the Intracoastal Waterway between Miami and Fort Lauderdale.

members of the different ethnic groups comprising the population. Florida is home to large numbers not only of blacks, but also Cubans and Latin Americans. In just the last five years, for example, some 80,000 Nicaraguans have fled the Sandinistas and come to Florida.

Just One Enormous Amusement Park?

Miami has long since overtaken New York as the "in city" of the western hemisphere. Miami is the new power base of the country. It is a city which more than any other embodies the American pioneering spirit – anything is possible, nothing is final, everyone has a chance. The Hispanics, especially, have seized their chance. In the "Casablanca of America", where only a few years ago civil war was threatening to break out, two languages are spoken, two cultures exist: Latin American and Anglo-Saxon – in that order.

Drugs are a part of Miami just as the Statue of Liberty is a part of New York. The annual turnover of the drug dealers is thought to be about six billion dollars – accumulating at 11,000 dollars per minute. The city authorities are trying to get the situation under control by carrying out weekly raids; successes are reported every day. Travellers, however, need not believe the horror stories they may have heard; they can explore Miami with complete peace of mind. The big drug deals are in any case presumably done behind closed doors in the glass palaces, and not on the streets.

Miami has not always been a traveller's paradise. At the beginning of the 1970s its popularity was on the wane. It had been superseded by the Côte d'Azur and the Caribbean – the one-time sunshine paradise was maligned as a has been, as "God's waiting room". The tourists had had enough of all the old people who were moving into run-down hotels to spend the winter. Nevertheless, the lull in tourism has long since swung back to a high; young Europeans and Japanese, in particular, have discovered Florida's "Gold Coast".

Florida's great appeal lies in the exceptional diversity of its landscapes, and its manmade attractions; in its many recreational and sporting facilities; in its climate and the lively, stimulating atmosphere which it owes to the population, with its strong Latin American element. Clever advertising long ago succeeded in making Florida attractive to tourists even in the hot and often stormy summer months, so that now it is high season all year round, which guarantees employment and ensures the onslaught of the masses.

In the swamplands of the Everglades, parts of which are still unexplored, it is possible to re-live the adventures of the American pioneering past in the midst of unspoilt nature. The pressure put on Washington by conservationsits has resulted in the huge area of wetland at the southern tip of the Florida peninsula being saved from drainage, thus keeping alive the only subtropical wilderness in the United States. Politicians and businessmen alike have recognised that untouched nature is also beneficial to the tourist trade. That is why the managers of Disney World have declared several thousand acres of their site to be a nature conservation area.

Although the sun shines every day in Florida and snow very rarely falls, there is nevertheless a dark cloud hovering over the state. Despite immense efforts on the part of conservationists, there is a danger that Florida is growing too quickly, that the crystal-clear spring waters are already too heavily polluted, that the greed for dollars is too great and that the state is becoming increasingly burdened with too many illegal immigrants. Further, one in four Americans over the age of sixty-five is packing up and moving to Florida. The southwest coast is being developed in another property and building boom. The stream of tourists is not drying up. There are well-founded fears that yet more animals will be exterminated, yet more land will be drained and yet more houses and pleasure parks will be built. Can a stop be enforced over this unrestricted growth, preserving the wonders of the state?

There are some encouraging signs that it can. Looking towards the next century, a new state constitution has been devised and written, incorporating strict laws against the pollution of the environment. From the state administration in Tallahassee have come announcements that more areas which have played a part in the history of Florida are to receive a protective status. Particular efforts to preserve cultural assets will be made in those places where there are thought to have been Spanish missions, Indian settlements and shipwrecks. Florida's inheritance is a rich one. Time will tell where the real value lies.

To see Florida as just one big amusement park or as a cultural desert of beaches does not do justice to it. For here the past and the future, fantasy and reality exist side by side in fascinating proximity. Here you can make your wildest dreams come true, you can search the coast for treasure which has lain undisturbed in the depths of the sea for centuries, and anyone who has experienced a sunrise here knows that the sun merely skims past the rest of the world and only truly rises over Florida.

SWAMP, SAND AND SEA
Reflections and Commentaries on the Sunshine State

Through its geographic location, Florida has been endowed with a unique climate and landscape; it is also distinguished by its superb natural beauty. Most visitors are left with a sense of illusion, as if they have seen a dreamland of the past in the Spanish architecture and nomenclature. But at the same time, Florida's romanticized commercialization and the seductively glamourous gangster way-of-life are reminders of the modern world. Our excerpts here will share with you some impressions gained by the tourists Alistair Cooke and Harriet Beecher Stowe along with the less admirable ways of life described by David Rieff. Visitors to Florida have always, or so it seems, been captivated by the natural wonders of the state, but at the same time Marjory Douglas reminds us of the devastating effects of a hurricane. The curiosity aroused in most northerners and the attempts to uncover and explore this vacation paradise are proof of the diversity and enchantment on offer to all who choose to partake.

Of Slaves ...

Who shall do the work for us? ... there are marshes to be drained, ... palmetto-plains to be grubbed up, and all under the torrid heats of a tropical sun.

"Chinese", say some; "Swedes," say others. "Germans," others.

But let us look at the facts before our face and eyes.

The thermometer, for these three days past, has risen over ninety every day. No white man that we know of dares stay in the fields later than ten o'clock: then he retires under shade to take some other and less-exposing work. The fine white sand is blistering hot: one might fancy that an egg would cook, as on Mt.

The Julia Tuttle Causeway is one of the main bridges between Miami and Miami Beach, where 120,000 hotel beds are waiting by the beach for weary travellers to lay their heads.

Vesuvius, by simply burying it in the sand. Yet the black laborers whom we leave in the field pursue their toil, if any thing, more actively, more cheerfully, than during the cooler months. The sun awakes all their vigor and all their boundless jollity. When their nooning time comes, they sit down not in the shade, but in some good hot place in the sand, and eat their lunch, and then stretch out, hot and comfortable, to take their noon siesta with the full glare of the sun upon them. Down in the swamp-land near our house we have watched old Simon as from hour to hour he drove his wheelbarrow, heavy with blocks of muck, up a steep bank, and deposited it. "Why, Simon!" we say: "how can you work so this hot weather?"

The question provokes an explosion of laughter. "Yah, hah, ho, ho, ho, misse! It be hot; dat so: ho, ho, ho!" ...

One tremendously hot day, we remember our steamer stopping at Fernandina. Owing to the state of the tide, the wharf was eight or ten feet above the boat; and the plank made a steep inclined plane, down which a mountain of multifarious freight was to be shipped on our boat. A gang of negroes, great, brawny, muscular fellows, seemed to make a perfect frolic of this job, which, under such a sun, would have threatened sunstroke to any white man. How they ran and shouted and jabbered, and sweated their shirts through, as one after another received on their shoulders great bags of cotton-seed, or boxes and bales; and ran down the steep plane with them into the boat! At last a low, squat giant of a fellow, with the limbs and muscles of a great dray-horse, placed himself in front of a large truck, and made his fellows pile it high with cotton-bags; then, holding back with a prodigious force, he took the load steadily down the steep plane till within a little of the bottom, when he dashed suddenly forward, and landed it half across the boat. This feat of gigantic strength he repeated again and again, running up each time apparently as fresh as if nothing had happened, shouting, laughing, drinking quarts of water, and sweating like a river-god. Never was harder work done in a more jolly spirit.

Now, when one sees such sights as these, one may be pardoned for thinking that the negro is the natural laborer of tropical regions. He is immensely strong; he thrives and flourishes physically under a temperature that exposes a white man to disease and death.

The malarial fevers that bear so hard on the white race have far less effect on the negro: it is rare that they have what are called here the "shakes;" and they increase and multiply, and bear healthy children, in situations where the white race deteriorate and grow sickly.

On this point we had an interesting conversation with a captain employed in the Government Coast Survey. The duties of this survey involve much hard labor, exposure to the fiercest extremes of tropical temperature, and sojourning and travelling in swamps and lagoons, often most deadly to the white race. For this reason, he manned his vessel with a crew composed entirely of negroes; and he informed us that the result had been perfectly satisfactory. The negro constitution enabled them to undergo with less suffering and danger the severe exposure and toils of the enterprise; and the gayety and good nature which belonged to the race made their toils seem to sit lighter upon them than upon a given number of white men. He had known them, after a day of heavy exposure, travelling through mud and swamps, and cutting saw-grass, which wounds like a knife, to sit down at evening, and sing songs and play on the banjo, laugh and tell stories, in the very best of spirits. He furthermore valued them for their docility, and perfect subjection to discipline. He announced strict rules, forbidding all drunkenness and profanity; and he never found a difficulty in enforcing these rules: their obedience and submission were perfect. When this gentleman was laid up with an attack of fever in St. Augustine, his room was beset by anxious negro mammies, relations of his men, bringing fruits, flowers, and delicacies of their compounding for "the captain".

HARRIET BEECHER STOWE (1811–1896) moved to Florida after the Civil War with the vague idea of assisting the newly emancipated slaves. The condescending views she expressed of the Negro workers were considered quite radical when they were written in 1873.

... and Seminoles

The Indians whom we call "Seminoles" today are of two groups. Both are immigrant stocks in Florida, where together they once occupied the whole state. These tribes are offshoots of the great Creek family, and while at first sight they look alike, they belong to two separate families, speak two different languages, and have little to do with each other.

After the long-drawn-out and incredibly expensive Seminole wars, the bulk of the Indians in Florida were gathered up and removed to the Indian Territory in Oklahoma, where, it must be admitted, they have done fairly well. But there was one band of men and women who eluded the United States troops for years, and, retreating farther and farther southward, finally maintained themselves and survived in the swamps. They have remained independent, refusing to have any dealings with the government of the United States.

Tarpon Springs, near St. Petersburg, is now known as the centre of sponge-diving. Greek immigrants brought this means of making a living from their native country, and made a new home for themselves here.

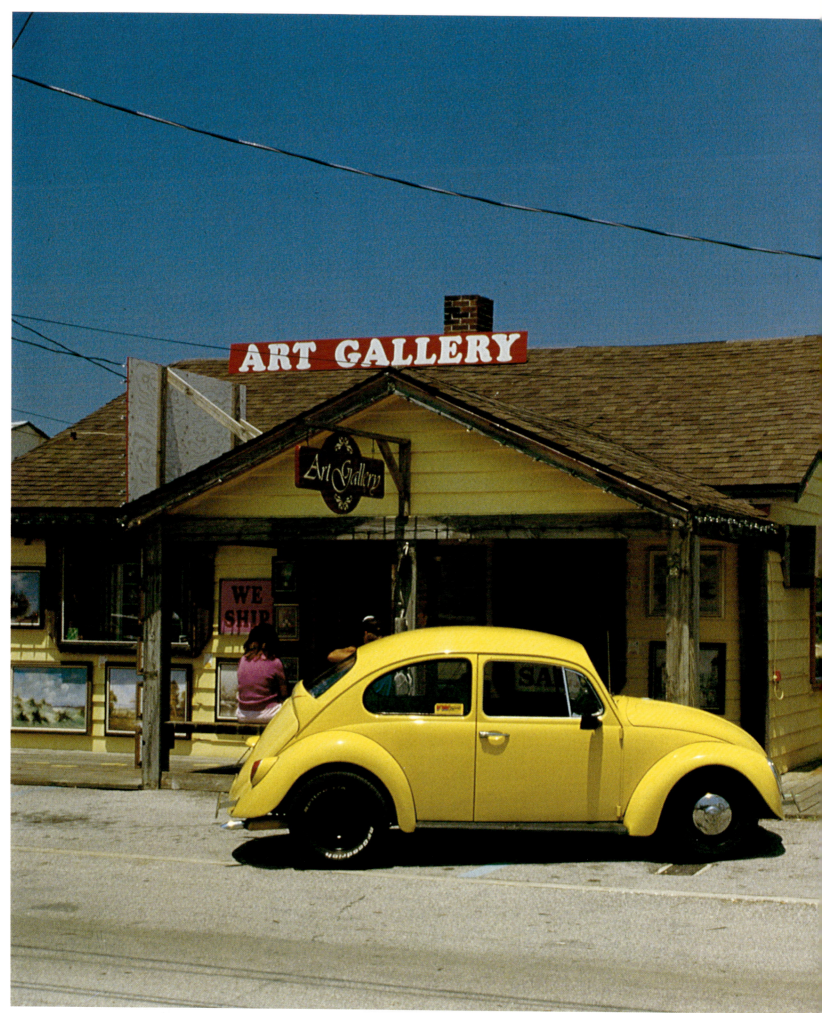
In the artists' quarter of John's Pass, near Clearwater, old buildings from elsewhere have been brought in and re-erected.

It is that remnant of the tribe which one sees in Florida today. Years ago I often saw old men, and especially old women, turn their backs on me contemptuously when I attempted to speak to them, or stare at me with a cool indifference which made me feel completely ashamed of what has happened to these people.

Unprotected by any treaty with the United States Government, the Seminoles have been driven into the most inaccessible and inhospitable swamps of South Florida. There they were content as long as there was enough water for their great, beautifully shaped cypress canoes to carry them about. Then the swamps were drained, and the Indians were left with almost no canoe lanes, and nowhere to travel except along the roadside ditch beside the Tamiami Trail. Homesteaders drove them from newly drained groves and fields to which the Seminoles' only title was the fact that they had cleared the land, and planted it, and used it for unnumbered years.

With the supply of game diminished, the Seminoles were forced by hunger to fall back on alligators, coons, and such disgusting fish as gars and grindles, which at times are about the only fish that can be secured in any quantity in the ditches. A few very old Indians living near the Dania Agency have received rations to the value of ten dollars a month, and two widows with children received fifteen dollars monthly a few years ago; but unlike many Western Indians, the Seminoles receive nothing from tribal funds or from Federal allotments, nor from the sale or rental of real property.

Under such conditions, inevitably tribal organization and authority have gradually weakened. The young men and girls are tempted to join the "Indian villages," where they are made a show for tourists. They are fed, to be sure, but also plied with liquor, and it is an unfortunate fact that these people have always been inordinately fond of alcohol. Venereal disease is, for the first time, making its appearance among the Indians.

For uncounted generations, the Seminoles have kept their blood very largely, if not absolutely, pure. I qualify this statement because, well within my own time, the Seminoles still had a few old Negro slaves who had been picked up as runaways before the Civil War. The women were taken into some of the chiefs' families, and some half-breed children resulted. But this small admixture of black blood is obviously disappearing. The last of the "slaves" was Hannah, who belonged to the family of Tallahassee and who lived until about 1900. There is no case on record where a Seminole woman has allied herself with a Negro man.

The danger of the Seminole nation is not the increase of Negro blood, but the attempts of

In Florida, leisure is catered for on a grand scale: jazz in Busch Gardens, the park belonging to one of the biggest breweries in the world (top), and attractions in the Magic Kingdom, the centerpiece of Disney World near Orlando (middle and bottom). Here, you can take a trip down the Congo River and thrill to scenes from the old pirate days ...

... And in the Magic Kingdom you can have your picture taken with the most famous mouse in the world (top), be driven around the grounds in period style (middle), or come face to face with pirates behind bars (bottom).

meandering white hunters and vagabonds to force their attentions on the Indian women when their men are away hunting. In the old days, if an Indian woman produced a bastard child, she was killed forthwith, but today the Indians are rather afraid to enforce the tribal law, because ignorant white sheriffs and their deputies are glad of a chance to put an Indian in jail.

After being long and widely regarded as one of the most strictly moral groups of people in the world, there is danger that the Seminoles may not be so any longer. The old men and women are deeply concerned lest their children become drunkards and beggars. It is a pity that the amusement parks which make a show of the Indians cannot be closed up by the Federal Government, but there is no way by which this can legally be done.

THOMAS BARBOUR wrote this essay on the conditions of Florida's Seminole Indians in 1945. A naturalist, Barbour's That Vanishing Eden *focuses on beauty of the state.*

The Hispanic Influence

Crime, looked at from a certain angle, is capitalism gone rococo. The real estate boom in the nineteen-twenties was certainly operatic in its unreality. Hearst's San Simeon would have fit in perfectly with the fake Spanish palaces the architect Addison Mizner was erecting in Palm Beach, Boca Raton, and Miami Beach. ...

Addison Mizner had always thought of himself as an architect, though whether he had actually ever qualified as one is open to question. Typically, when his credentials were reviewed by a Florida state licensing board, the examiners allowed Addison to skip the "technical" parts of the exam. But even if he didn't know how he did what he did, his talent is undeniable. Addison Mizner's buildings were described by Alva Johnston in his brilliant book about the Mizner brothers as "the Bastard-Spanish-Moorish-Romanesque-Gothic-Renaissance-Bull-Market-Damn-The-Expense style," and they were the perfect embodiment of that protean ostentation which marked the boom. It was crazy, it was ridiculous, but somehow everyone was taken in. Sort of like buying land in a swamp, that prototypical boom exercise in credulousness with a capital C lampooned only a few years later in the Marx Brothers' film about Florida, The Coconuts.

No dreams were too grandiose for the developers, for if they hadn't been grandiose everyone would have noticed that this wasn't the south of France or Andalusia, but a mangrove swamp one hundred forty miles from Cuba. Partly it was the shills who kept things

Private villas line the New River in Fort Lauderdale. The "Venice of Florida" is criss-crossed by a network of canals.

going – Damon Runyon wrote advertising copy for South Florida land. But mostly it was just sheer, mad gall. In Boca Raton, which was meant to be the new Venice, Mizner dubbed the main road which led to his house "El Camino Real". Spain and Italy were always getting confused: it must have been those actinic rays. His brother Wilson actually proposed to the Boca Raton corporation that Venetian gondoliers be imported to ply the canal which ran alongside this royal road. Alva Johnston wrote tartly that if the Florida boom had gone on much longer than it did, there wouldn't have been a tile roof left anywhere in southern Spain.

The modern Florida of Epcot Center and Disney World is only the latest turn on the old Florida fantasy; everything is a theme park; every place is really someplace else, or can be if you want it to be badly enough. Consider the case of the city of Coral Gables. This was another Shangri-la built on the failure of an agricultural investment. In the eighteen-nineties, a minister from Gaines, New York, Solomon Merrick, abandoned his flock and came down to Miami to start up a citrus plantation. When it went bust, his son George came up with the idea of Coral Gables. The Merricks made $150,000,000 the first year. ...

In Coral Gables, the streets are called Ponce de Leon, Alhambra, Cordoba, Almeria, Toledo, Alcazar, and on and on, mapping Iberia over again. The comedy of these decisions is that today they actually mean something. One is no longer talking about yet another Florida theme park, but rather of a city in which the majority of the people are Spanish-speaking. They know how to pronounce these names that have a significance wholly other than what was originally intended. I noticed this first when I saw that Anglos in Miami refer to "Ponce de Leon" as if talking about an English panderer, while Cubans pronounce each syllable with all conveyable delight, authentically.

The significance of these street names that identify Miami as a physical entity for the visitor, the resident, and the immigrant alike is profound. One drunken evening in Miami, Heberto Padilla, perhaps the finest Cuban poet of his generation, who now lives in exile in Miami, rhapsodized over the eerie predestination implicit in the street names of Coral Gables. "They did not expect," he said, as we weaved, our arms linked like parading bullfighters, through the mock Spanish castle-gate that guards and identifies the entrance to Coral Gables, "they did not expect the invasion of all of us, of we barbarian Spaniards. But we are here."

Suddenly it seemed that Miami, without having earned over time a tragic history, had had one grafted on itself by migration. The real connection to the past in South Florida ought to be with the Seminole Wars. Instead, developers came to a wild place, invented an image of Moorish Spain complete with all the modern conveniences only to find, fifty years later, that a real variant, a cutting from Moorish Spain, had in fact arrived. History had arrived aboard those refugee flights from Varadero Airport in Havana in the early nineteen-sixties. And unlike Los Angeles or the other great cities of the American Southwest in which, with every passing day, Mexican and Central American immigrants seem more and more to predominate, there was no organic connection to speak of between Miami and Hispanic America. For there was, first of all, no Miami. Beyond this, California, New Mexico, Arizona, Texas – these are the lost provinces of Mexico, never completely cut off from their Hispanic roots. But Miami? Miami was and is an invented vision, a fantasy of ideal living. It is, as Jackie Gleason called it, "the sun and fun capital of the world." In other words, it is a whim of its real estate developers. What was it doing now, I asked myself, caught up in this Spanish tragedy, this fiery node which now links the Americas?

The changing face of Miami is here described by the twentieth century author DAVID RIEFF.

The 1920s

When I came back to Florida in 1920, after the First World War, it was because I belonged there, although my mind was stretched to wider horizons. The wonderful light, the incomparable sea were the same. The state had changed; the war had brought a sharp end to its sleepy, nineteenth-century flavor. Miami bustled with more people, more building, more business. There was a new causeway to Miami Beach, where the palm trees were taller: there were shops on Lincoln Road and a few hotels and Carl Fisher's new casino and swimming pool.

I was now my father's associate editor with a column of my own, to fill with attempts at verse and book reviews and comments for which, within reason, I had a free hand. But perhaps at first my mind was too full of the beauties of the old cities I had seen, Paris and Venice and Athens, not to see that already the growing city was not treasuring its own great natural advantages. ...

There was a little boom in land, in 1920, which changed quickly to a depression in which new building stopped. Men back from the war went away to find jobs. But as the Prohibition Act of that January suddenly roused a nationwide demand for liquor, a flood of more adventurous, less scrupulous men began rumrunning in speed boats from Nassau or Havana to the long Florida coasts, forever a haven for smugglers.

Tallahassee, the capital of Florida, makes up for its small-town character with its university and many summer festivals.

Spectacular animal shows are among the main attractions in the wide range of leisure activities on offer in Florida – a dolphin show in the Sea World amusement center in Orlando. Flipper came from Florida ...

From hundreds of beaches or waterways fast liquor-laden cars roared up the long roads to inland cities or out of the state. A new season opened in the fall of 1920 with visitors crowding in to spend war profits at the new race track, at expensive night clubs with docks for liquor cargoes and every sort of gambling, with a great increase of prostitution. Graft and corruption began to reach into politics and city government.

Much more quietly the Ku Klux Klan, reactivated nationally in 1915 and with a Klan demagogue elected governor in Tallahassee, forced even the pettiest city officeholders, in fear of losing their jobs, to join in their hooded processions through alarmed colored towns and to take part in cross burnings and beatings in country districts. In Miami winter visitors were not allowed to employ Negro chauffeurs. Respectable Negro tradesmen were forced out of business. A Negro dance orchestra at one of the hotels had to leave town. There were no lynchings in the city but a crippled English Episcopal missionary to Bahama Negroes was tarred and feathered one night and dumped ... nearly dead on the main street. Neither paper mentioned the incident and no public protest was made.

In Tallahassee, sent to cover the inauguration of the governor elected to follow the Ku Klux Klan governor, I found everything much as it always had been: political hangers-on talking loud in the lobby of the old Leon Hotel and a gala tide of politicians, their wives and daughters, dancing triumphantly at the inaugural ball among the cases of old battle flags and dim portraits in the Capitol. It could not have seemed more distant to the new life of Florida. ...

In Miami again, I found myself involved in two different worlds. One was made up of stimulating people from everywhere, with trained, intelligent and keen minds; old residents newly discovered by me, new residents and visitors. Their enthusiasm gave me a new awareness of this wonderful tropical region of south Florida; John C. Gifford, nationally known forester and ecologist who for years lectured about the necessity of planting tropical trees and building airy tropical houses; Charles Torrey Simpson, the grand old Florida naturalist, David Fairchild, chief plant explorer, who set up the Plant Introduction Garden on Brickell Avenue for the U.S. Department of Agriculture, and with his wife, Marian Bell Fairchild, made his estate in Coconut Grove a meeting place for visiting scientists; ...

My other life, a very disturbing one, began when my father heard a speaker at the newly established Rotary Club luncheon say there were children in Miami whose

... And Sea Aquarium in Miami goes one better: here they feature an act with trained killer whales. Until very recently they were believed to be untamable.

parents could not afford to give them milk and asked me to set up the "Herald Baby Milk Fund." It was the first public charity. The investigations gave me a shocking view of the city, still so new, but already with run-down old houses crammed with misery. Nothing was to be said of the needs of Negro babies, but I became increasingly aware of the extension, just beyond the outworn white districts, of the long, dismal sandy streets of colored town, with all its festering problems; no running water except one standpipe for perhaps thirty houses; no inside toilets, but only dirt privies; and landlords who removed the front doors of houses on Saturday night if the weekly rent was not paid. My father, as judge of the local police court, was fighting all that also, ordering landlords arrested for permitting filthy and run-down conditions. But the law did not allow fines of more than $50 apiece, which they were glad to pay rather than spend a cent for repairs or improvements. There were no organizations then to help these unfortunate families in other ways, family welfare, employment, counseling, and I was not allowed to write about the need for more kinds of assistance. But such needs were unimportant to the growing and more prosperous tourist city. I grew more and more discouraged. ...

When I went back that fall of 1923 I was changed, steadied and reinforced. But the city was changed even more. There was excitement in the air, an exhilaration in men's faces and speech, as if what they had ardently hoped for was actually coming true at last. Lots were selling everywhere, new buildings going up, the newspaper was busier and bigger, new people were coming in with money, eager to make more money. It was the beginning of that extraordinary time when people from everywhere acted as if gold in millions was to be picked up in Miami streets, the Miami boom, the Florida boom, of 1923 to 1926.

Sales of lots at Carl Fisher's Miami Beach, reached by a new causeway, with new hotels, night clubs, polo fields, casinos, began to increase. But the boom really began when George Merrick opened up for sale the lots in Coral Gables, on 3,000 acres of grove and pineland west of town. It was the first completely planned city in the state, if not in the country, streets and boulevards planted with trees, canals and bridges, fountains, entrance gates, Spanish residences in gardens, a big swimming pool, golf links, hotels, a carefully zoned business district. His advertising echoed throughout the country. He opened elaborate sales offices everywhere, brought down prospective buyers by trainloads.

Processions of decorated cars, with brass bands, swept them out to the great daily auctions by a famous auctioneer. Rumors of his first week's sales mounted into millions. ...

The fever of speculation seemed to have slackened in Miami and Miami Beach in the winter of 1925. The hot summer of 1926 was completely dull.

The hurricane that struck the Florida peninsula on that September night had surged, with little or no warning, from far across the Atlantic, increasing its enormous vicious whirl in a blur of winds and rains and rising ominous storm tides. It struck the expanded city, vulnerable with flimsy boom-time buildings, real estate shacks, garages, with the explosive force of a vast bomb. All night long the screaming of incredible winds of more than 125 miles an hour deafened the noises of falling trees, collapsing walls, breaking glass, torn-away roofs, as the driven tides burst over the bay front and the low grounds, driving ships aground, boats into houses, and leaving debris everywhere.

When by morning light the hurricane seemed to have stopped abruptly hundreds of stunned people poured out of their beleaguered and broken houses to climb, staring, over wreck-filled streets. They were caught there when the wall of steely winds and rain at the other side of the calm center, which few people had ever heard of, moved across to blot them out again. People by the score were killed and injured. When the last of the hurricane had roared away on its terrible course the city seemed in ruins. Across the little towns about Okeechobee, where hundreds drowned, all the way across once-booming Florida, the path of destruction and of death lay steaming under the next day's sun.

The boom ended with that shocking outburst of weather. The people of Miami who were left struggled out of their wild and impossible dreams of riches to face the ruin together, an aroused, sobered and unified community.

Help poured in from all over the country. There was work for everyone, clearing, cleaning, repairing, rebuilding. Some men who had been millionaires stayed to take what jobs they could get, running elevators, going back to farming, rebuilding their deserted businesses, fishing. To clear up the chaos and confusion left by the avalanche of worthless boom paper was the work of years. Its new building code, strictly adapted to hurricanes, became a model for the whole state and later for the whole hurricane-haunted Atlantic coast.

The Minnesota-born writer MARJORY STONEMAN DOUGLAS was very familiar with life in the South, particularly Florida where she eventually settled. This excerpt is taken from her 1967 text Florida: The Long Frontier.

Key West

He did not take the bicycle but walked down the street. The moon was up now and the trees were dark against it, and he passed the frame houses with their narrow yards, light coming from the shuttered windows; the unpaved alleys, with their double rows of houses; Conch town, where all was starched, well-shuttered, virtue, failure, grits and boiled grunts, undernourishment, prejudice, righteousness, interbreeding and the comforts of religion; the open-doored, lighted Cuban bolito houses, shacks whose only romance was their names; The Red House, Chicha's; the pressed stone church; its steeples sharp ugly triangles against the moonlight; the big grounds and the long, black-domed bulk of the convent, handsome in the moonlight; a filling station and a sandwich place, bright-lighted beside a vacant lot where a miniature golf course had been taken out; past the brightly lit main street with the three drug stores, the music store, the five Jew stores, three pool rooms, two barbershops, five beer joints, three ice cream parlours, the five poor and the one good restaurant, two magazine and paper places, four second-hand joints (one of which made keys), a photographer's, an office building with four dentists' offices upstairs, the big dime store, a hotel on the corner with taxis opposite; and across, behind the hotel, to the street that led to jungle town, the big unpainted frame house with lights and the girls in the doorway, the mechanical piano going, and a sailor sitting in the street; and then on back, past the back of the brick courthouse with its clock luminous at half-past ten, past the whitewashed jail building shining in the moonlight, to the embowered entrance of the Lilac Time where motor cars filled the alley.

The Lilac Time was brightly lighted and full of people, and as Richard Gordon went in he saw the gambling room was crowded, the wheel turning and the little ball clicking brittle against metal partitions set in the bowl, the wheel turning slowly, the ball whirring, then clicking jumpily until it settled and there was only the turning of the wheel and the rattling of chips. At the bar, the proprietor who was serving with two bartenders, said "Allo." Allo, Mist' Gordon. What you have?"

ERNEST HEMINGWAY (1899–1961) used his adopted home of Key West as the setting for several texts. His 1937 novel To Have and Have Not *focuses on the running of rum and revolutionaries from Cuba to the Florida Keys during the Depression.*

The old Capitol building in Tallahassee housed the government of Florida from 1845 to the end of the 1970s. Behind the old building is the new seat of the administration of the "Sunshine State".

The first Tarzan films were shot on the Wakulla River.

The wealth of species to be found in the Everglades manifests itself in the bird life: a young brown pelican (left) and a white egret (right).

The Quest for Sun

To most of us, though, who know a tree as something with leaves, the winter is a thing to be endured. True, we have lots of sunshine and there is an exhilaration in the sharp light and the crunching snows. But come November, and again in February and March, we wish we were somewhere else. We get up in the morning and stumble over to the window and look at the thermometer on the outside to know what to wear when we get outside. I realize, if I recall my European homes correctly, that it is an American's privilege to wake in the morning and slosh around naked without knowing what the weather's like outside. But comfort, like cocaine, demands an increasing dosage. And by December it is not enough to be warm indoors and cold out. It would be nice to be warm all the time. So for Americans with money saved, no matter what their kind or class ("income group" as we airily say) December is the month that suggests one beckoning word – Florida. It is the time when the rich, the comfortably idle, the alimony-plated divorcée, the Midwest farmer with his crops in, the tired performers in a circus troupe, the business executive with a couple of weeks' holiday in hand, the exceptional show-girl bored with the nightly routine on Broadway, the well-heeled black-marketeer, the leisured grandmother and the grandchildren she dotes on, the cab-driver about to switch employers, the gangster and the race-track tout – all of them abed at night dream the same dream and see themselves lying in not much more than a coat of golden tan on a gypsum beach, the sand fine as sugar, the lapping sea of a shining aquamarine. You will detect a slight sneer in the tone of this account of the people who are off to Florida, and I hope you will interpret it correctly as nothing more than envy.

Ponce de Leon, the first white man to touch the Florida coast, in 1513, thought he would find there the fountain of youth. And De Soto, twenty-six years later, went looking for gold. Four hundred years later, in a nation which clings to its youth more than any other nation, the daydream of the winter visitor is much the same. And the centuries shake hands in the spectacle of an aging Midwestern farmer and his wife driving southeast in a De Soto car, or a show-girl off on the night train for Miami and a little private project of her own, from which digging for gold is not excluded.

It would depress a Floridian to hear me approach his state in this, the condescending Northern, way. For to most Americans Florida is not a state but a state of mind,

The crocodile, along with the flamingo, is one of the symbols of Florida. The crocodile had to be placed under protection, because it was on the verge of being wiped out completely. This specimen was snapped in the Busch Gardens Zoo.

not a place to live at all but a place to work off a year's inhibitions in a few determined weeks of pleasure. But Florida itself is a little to blame for this reputation. Though it has a great trade in citrus fruit, and a developing cattle-market, a cigar industry, and a wealth of what Americans call folkways, it boasts that its most marketable commodity is its climate. And it spends millions of dollars a year describing that climate in print in the hope of attracting, and attracting back, into the state several score million dollars' worth of winter tourists. As early as 1910 a newspaper in St. Petersburg, on the west coast of the peninsula, offered to give away its whole daily edition any time in the year when the sun failed to shine before three in the afternoon. They have had to pay the forfeit no more than four or five times a year.

The English-born writer ALISTAIR COOKE first visited the United States in 1932. He is one of England's best-known commentators on life in America. This excerpt is taken from Cooke's 1953 text One Man's America.

Eternal Springs

I have always thought that we were owed some further explanation about Ponce de León and his search for the Fountain of Youth. Who planted in his head the idea that there was such a thing? He was supposed to have made his first search in Bimini. That was a mighty poor guess from any angle. But Florida is another story, and certainly a far better bet as a hunting ground, for North Central Florida has more spectacular, indeed more incredible, springs than any other region of which I have ever heard. It is impossible here to describe these springs in detail, but it can truthfully be said that, like the stars, one differeth from another in glory.

My first choice is Wakulla, not simply because at times it is probably the largest spring in the entire world, but because there is a sense of timelessness and mystery which is overwhelming as you row about its pellucid waters. It is a unique experience to look down and see the remains of a mastodon (its mate now stands in the State Museum at Tallahassee) lying in clear sight on the bottom of the spring (although pretty well encrusted with limestone), and a bee tree obviously chopped open by the stone axes of primitive people using the tools of untold generations ago. The spring, which is really a crystal lake in the woods, spews forth a river which winds through a lovely stand of cypress. And, since it belongs to the du Ponts, a family appreciative of beauty, it has been kept unsullied.

Here as one looks into this strange and mysterious world, one sees a bewildering variety of aquatic vegetation which sways and waves in the swift stream and through which the usual swarms of fish and turtles, snakes and alligators, wander about, pushing aside the moving plants in a strange, fairylike land under water. The water itself is so limpid that you can get no concept of depth by peering down into it and you may stick your arm down to touch a turtle and find you could not reach him with a ten-foot pole. On the shores there are birds beyond number. Here, as far as I know, is the one great concentration of limpkins remaining in Florida. ...

In summer in this part of Florida it is hotter than the hinges of Gehenna and we had to keep our windows open to breathe. You will probably think that I am a monument of mendacity when I say that the chorus of frogs of perhaps twenty species completely prevented sleep. It would have been as easy to sleep in a boiler mill or a drop-forge foundry. However, the early morning ride in the glass-bottomed boat over the great chasm, where crystal-clear water boiled forth from an enormous depth, was rewarding. I believe that, were not the throat from which the water pours curved on its route underground, it would have been possible to see down more than two hundred feet.

Two hundred thousand gallons a minute issue from this magic well. On the morning of our visit, the amphibian chorus died off with the rising of the sun and the only sounds were the plop, plop, plop of the jumping mullet and the calls of the awakening birds. Mullet constantly run up the Wakulla River from salt water, in great numbers – whether for a change of scene or for medicinal reasons I have no way of telling.

The outlet of Silver Springs is the famous and lovely Oklawaha River. Years ago stern-wheel steamers from Jacksonville used to reach the spring by way of this stream and the St. Johns River. It has been known to pour forth five hundred million gallons a day in the rainy season – enough water to supply the city of New York.

It has now become a tourist resort visited by tens of thousands and unfortunately shows the result of its commercialization. Here you may be photographed sitting astride "Ferdinand" – not a bull, but a great fat ox, on the very shore of the springs; or eat a fried chicken near its bank; or watch some obviously unhappy Indians, far from home, do beadwork and make various sorts of objects for sale.

DR. THOMAS BARBOUR spent his life exploring every corner of Florida. His descriptions of this state are both a plea for the preservation of the natural beauty and an expression of regret and anger at the careless destruction of this ecological paradise.

Alligator Fishing

It was by this time dusk, and the alligators had nearly ceased their roar, when I was again alarmed by a tumultuous noise that seemed to be in my harbor and therefore engaged my immediate attention. Returning to my camp, I found it undisturbed and then continued on to the extreme point of the promontory, where I saw a scene, new and surprising, which at first threw my senses into such a tumult, that it was some time before I could comprehend what was the matter. However, I soon accounted for the prodigious assemblage of crocodiles at this place, which exceeded everything of the kind I had ever heard of ...

... The river (in this place), from shore to shore and perhaps near half a mile above and below me, appeared to be one solid bank of fish of various kinds, pushing through to his narrow pass of St. Juan's into the little lake on their return down the river, and ... the alligators were in such incredible numbers and so close together from shore to shore that it would have been easy to have walked across on their heads, had the animals been harmless. What expressions can sufficiently declare the shocking scene that for some minutes contiued, whilst this mighty army of fish were forcing the pass? During this attempt, thousands, I may say hundreds of thousands, of them were caught and swallowed by the devouring alligators. I have seen an alligator take up out of the water several great fish at a time, and just squeeze them betwixt his jaws, while the tails of the great trout flapped about his eyes and lips, ere he had swallowed them. The horrid noise of their closing jaws, their plunging amidst the broken banks of fish and rising with their prey some feet upright above the water, the floods of water and blood rushing out of their mouths, and the clouds of vapor issuing from their wide nostrils were truly frightful. This scene continued at intervals during the night, as the fish came to the pass. After this sight, shocking and tremendous as it was, I found myself somewhat easier and more reconciled to my situation; being convinced that their extraordinary assemblage here was owing to the annual feast of fish; and that they were so well employed in their own element that I had little occasion to fear their paying me a visit.

WILLIAM BARTRAM (1739–1823) was the son of the famous American botanist John Bartram. A naturalist himself, Bartram and his father explored the St. John's River along the east coast of Florida by canoe in 1765–1766. Bartram's Travels through North and South Carolina, Georgia, East and West Florida, *published in 1791, was immensely popular in North America and Europe.*

The Great Blue Heron finds living conditions ideal in the mangrove thickets; this one is near Wakulla Springs not far from Tallahassee.

Miami Beach – at the beginning of the century deep in the wilderness, now one of Florida's major tourist attractions.

The pot of gold at the end of the rainbow: Miami Beach, retirement home for America's more affluent pensioners.

Miami-Style Crime

The Miami Beach one visits today, despite both the improvements and the depredations of time, is still recognizable as the place those real estate hucksters fashioned out of swamp, grove, and bay bottom. All the clichés about the good life, the persistent harping on the fineness of the weather, the boosterism that makes Texas high school football look like a get-together at a Carthusian monastery, had their start in the South Florida of the nineteen-twenties. For the cocaine cowboys of today, sipping champagne in the private clubs and tasting rooms of Coconut Grove, the nineteen-thirties could provide no less a figure than Al Capone, the first of many mobsters to find Miami copacetic both for business and pleasure. Fisher had created two "residential" islands along the causeway, Palm and Hibiscus. Capone bought a house on Palm. Even the most recent arrivals to Miami, people for whom the name Flagler presents considerable elocutionary difficulties, know this. Haitian cabdrivers, fresh off the boat, will point the place out. Some even mention that the great Caruso ... was brought to Miami specially to sing for Capone. There is even, discreetly, Capone iconography. Recently, a cocaine ring in Miami was busted by the cops. The gang had been living in incredible ostentation, even by the Borgia-like standards of Dade County. They had dozens of cars, spent thousands each night on restaurants and girls, raced "cigarette" speedboats in Biscayne Bay, and didn't kill too many people. They were bound to be caught; they had none of the stoical patience of pros in for the long haul: it was all too flamboyant, too much like a movie. Indeed, it was as if these men weren't able to distinguish any longer between the lives they were living and a movie they were starring in.

The ringleader had been a national bicycle champion in Cuba, leaving during the Mariel boatlift of 1980. When the police (not the Basile-clothed glamour boys of TV's "Miami Vice," but the underpaid, out-gunned husbands and fathers of the real Miami Vice Squad, whose annual budget is only slightly more than one episode of the TV series) raided his office, they found behind his desk a poster of Al Pacino in his role as the coke dealer in the film Scarface. When I told this story to a friend who knows the cocaine trade, he sighed. «In my day," he said, "we would have had a picture of a real guy. We would have had Al Capone."

The contemporary author DAVID RIEFF provides an incisive description of Miami's criminal elements.

Evening mood over the Intracoastal Waterway near Turnberry Isle in the southeast of Florida.

FLORIDA
CONCISE TRAVEL GUIDE

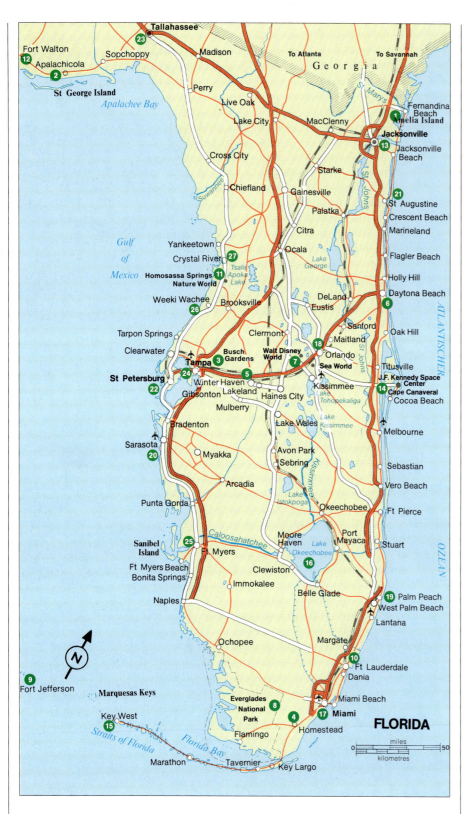

southwest. In 1988 the population of Florida numbered slightly less than thirteen million people, with roughly thirty percent of them black. There is also a sizeable Hispanic minority in the state. Florida was discovered by Juan Ponce de León at Easter (*Pascua Florida* in Spanish) in the year 1513, and was claimed for Spain. It has been part of the territory of the United States since 1821, and in 1845 become the twenty-seventh state in the union. The state capital is Tallahassee.

Because it is warmer and sunnier than anywhere else in the country, Florida became known as the "Sunshine State". The winters are mild (in Miami, in the south, the temperature never falls below 68 degrees Fahrenheit/20 degrees Celsius), the summers are hot and sultry; short-lived storms are to be expected every day.

Most of Florida lies within the Eastern Time zone (five hours behind Greenwich Mean Time). Only the extreme northwest, the part of the panhandle to the west of Apalachicola, falls within the Central Time zone (six hours behind Greenwich Mean Time). Throughout North America, as in Europe, the clocks are put forward an hour from the end of April to the beginning of November (Daylight Saving Time, or DST).

POINTS OF INTEREST

AMELIA ISLAND ①. The dozen or so miles of sandy beaches along this peninsula on the northeastern coast of Florida are generally empty. Amelia Island is the only place in the United States which in the course of its history has flown eight different flags: French, Spanish, English, Mexican and Confederates forces and other armies have all fought over the peninsula during the last four hundred years, before it finally became part of the United States of America in 1821.

The largest town of Amelia Island is Fernandina Beach; the old part of the town has been put on the list of American cultural assets worthy of protection. In the Old Quarter, which consists of thirty streets, there are distinguished Victorian villas, Queen Anne style houses, and other buildings whose architecture is labelled, rather disparagingly, "Steamboat Gothic".

The numbers in circles refer to the map, those in italics refer to colour photographs.

GENERAL INFORMATION

The Florida peninsula, bordering on Georgia and Alabama, is approximately 465 miles/750 kilometres long and covers an area of some 58,650 square miles/151,940 square kilometres. This southernmost state of the United States stretches south between the Atlantic Ocean and the Gulf of Mexico. From its southern tip a chain of coral islands – the Florida Keys – trails away to the

FLORIDA
CONCISE TRAVEL GUIDE

APALACHICOLA ②. This fishing village on the northwest coast of Florida is famous for its superb oysters. The fishermen use punting poles to steer their little boats out into the shallow sea. Around the fishermen's huts shells are piled up waist high, and there are sacks of mussels on all the boat docks. The excellent seafood can be sampled in "raw bars" along the quayside.

In Apalachicola there is a museum dedicated to one John Gorrie. We might not be familiar with the name, but we owe a lot to John Gorrie. He was a doctor who wanted to make the heat more bearable for his malaria patients, and so he invented a machine for cooling the air – the forerunner of air conditioning. He needed ice to cool the air, but at that time ice had to be shipped down from Canada, and this was expensive and impractical, so he then invented an ice-making machine and the refrigerator, patenting both inventions. It was not until long after his death in 1851, however, that his inventions were properly appreciated. Replicas of his machines can be seen in the John Gorrie Museum; the originals are in the Smithsonian Institute in Washington.

BUSCH GARDENS ③, to the north of Tampa, is Florida's biggest attraction after Disney World and Sea World. Like a lot of other things in Florida, its story began in a modest way. In the beginning, in the early 1970s, there was a brewery where each visitor, on leaving, was given three bottles of beer as a promotional gift. In order that the visitors would not have to drink their beer standing up, the brewers put benches and tables in the garden, where flamingoes had free range and parrots squawked in the trees. Then the Busch family built the Old Swiss Restaurant and extended the gardens, where they then also began keeping giraffes, zebras, elephants, buffaloes, gazelles and white Bengal tigers. The last enclosure was opened in the summer of 1988, since which time white-headed eagles and golden eagles have also had their nests here.

Today, Busch Gardens, with its much admired botanical jungle garden in which more than three thousand animals can be seen, is the fourth largest zoo in the United States. As part of its clever advertising strategy, the Busch

At the entrance to Busch Gardens, combining a zoo, botanical garden and brewery.

dynasty has in the meantime renamed the zoo "The Dark Continent". There is a Serengeti Plain and a Lake Tanganyika; the farm is called Nairobi. In the Timbuktu Hospitality House, built in the style of a foreign legion outpost, a permanent beer festival is held. *4/5, 28, 41*

CARTOON MUSEUM. For twenty-two years, the owner has been collecting cartoons, comic books and comic magazines from all over the world. Valuable items, such as complete runs of Asterix, first editions of Prince Valiant, and Superman comics in Chinese, are displayed behind glass. Also on display are hundreds of precious original drawings by famous cartoonists, which demonstrate how the figures were created and given movement. The futuristic science fiction comics are also represented in the collection. The Cartoon Museum can be found at 4300 South Semoran Boulevard in Orlando ⑱.

CORAL CASTLE. The unrequited love of a man for a woman led to the building of Coral Castle in Homestead ④, thirty-seven miles/sixty kilometres south of Miami. Between 1925 and 1940, Edward Leedskalnin, a Latvian, built this castle of coral limestone without help from anyone. He claimed to know the secret of how the Egyptians built their pyramids. Perhaps he really did know how boulders weighing several tons were moved in those days. Whether he did or not, this eccentric built everything of stone: furniture, a sundial, towers, pyramids and countless love tokens, such as a stone heart weighing some five thousand tons. Note particularly the double doors, weighing nine tons, which swing open at a mere touch. Apparently no one has ever found out how the lovelorn émigré managed to build this curiosity.

CYPRESS GARDENS. Florida's oldest pleasure park, lies to the south of Orlando at Winter Haven ⑤. In 1930 the Pope family began to create a botanical garden on the banks of the idyllic Lake Eloise, and today the gardens have grown into a tropical jungle. Visitors are transported silently by electrically powered boats through a canal system, while a guide tells them about some of the nine thousand plant species which have been planted here. The old cypress trees, heavily draped in Spanish moss, are interesting. The births of a two-toed sloth and a dwarf hippopotamus, extremely rare occurrences in captivity, have attracted the attention of zoologists. In Animal Forest, children are allowed to ride on giant tortoises and stroke the animals.

The main attractions are the daily water skiing show, featuring among other things a four-tier human pyramid circling in perfect formation, and the fire-divers, blazing human torches who

FLORIDA
CONCISE TRAVEL GUIDE

dive to safety in the water. Here, too, can be seen the only ice skating show in Florida.

DAYTONA BEACH ⑥, on Florida's east coast, is a city of speed records, motor racing and students. Once the motor manufacturers Henry Ford, Louis Chevrolet and Ransom Olds had discovered that car tyres leave hardly any trace on the hard-packed sand of Daytona Beach, thirteen records were set here between 1902 and 1935. Driving is still permitted on the sands of Daytona Beach, but with a speed restriction of ten miles/twenty kilometres per hour. Highspeed racing has been banished from the beach, and it now takes place inland on concrete racetracks. It gets a little crowded in Daytona Beach in March and April: that is when students from all over the country gather for "Spring Break", an eight-week party with open-air concerts and games on the beach. At the beginning of March, half-a-million motorcycle fans also descend on the town for Daytona Supercross. When they arrive, you can no longer see the sand for bikes.

DISNEY WORLD ⑦. Over the last thirty years, what was once a huge area of swampland to the southwest of Orlando has become the centre of an area visited by more tourists, from every part of the world, than any other amusement park on earth. Mickey Mouse and his companions draw millions of visitors every year. Donald Duck the banker is pleased about it, he even has his own currency in circulation: the Disney Dollar, bearing the smiling face of Mickey Mouse, can actually be used to pay for purchases (that is, if you would not rather take it home as a souvenir). Every single one of the 25,000 employees of Disney World is under a contractual obligation to be friendly to the visitors: the well-oiled machine has to work smoothly. And when you leave, you are sent on your way with a smile and a "come back soon".

The centrepiece of Disney's world of plastic is the Magic Kingdom, with its Main Street US, a replica of a nineteenth century American street. Along Main Street you will find a town hall, silent movie cinemas, banks and houses, with wooden sidewalks connecting them all;

Top: One of the main attractions in Cypress Gardens is the water skiing show.
Bottom: A monorail runs between the Magic Kingdom and Epcot Center.

you get the strange feeling that you have seen it all before.

The 100-acre/40-hectare park, with its forty-five attractions, is split up into different theme areas. The main attractions are Pirates of the Caribbean, the Jungle Cruise, It's a Small World, the submarine trip 20,000 Leagues Under the Sea, and the nerve-racking Space Mountain rollercoaster. Every day of the year there is a big parade along Main Street and in front of Cinderella's Castle. On summer evenings you can enjoy the Electric Light Parade and fireworks over the castle. *28, 29*

EPCOT CENTRE. In the early 1960s Walt Disney, the brilliant designer and creator of Mickey Mouse, drew up plans for a city of the future, which he named "Experimental Prototype Community of Tomorrow". It was to be an enclosed city with no air pollution, accommodating 200,000 people, and it was to be sited near Orlando ⑱.

When, after Disney's death in 1966, his partners took over the running of the production company, this project was abandoned and the Epcot Centre was turned into a theme park. In collaboration with futurologists and

FLORIDA
CONCISE TRAVEL GUIDE

space experts, they designed a display showing the world of today (World Showcase) and the world of tomorrow (Future World).

In the World Showcase, architectural styles and products from eleven different countries are on display. Highlights of Future World include The Land, showing the vegetation zones of the world and agricultural technologies of the future, and The Living Seas, where there is an ocean behind glass, complete with sharks and thousands of other marine creatures. In the Universe of Energy, you can travel in solar-powered carriages through the prehistoric age of the dinosaurs. And finally, Horizons offers an interesting glimpse into the twenty-first century, answering the question of what our living and working conditions be like then.

EVERGLADES NATIONAL PARK ⑧. Fifty miles/eighty kilometres south of Miami, outside Florida City, is the entrance (and museum) of the Everglades National Park, which occupies almost the whole of the southern tip of Florida, covering an area of more than 2,300 square miles/6,000 square kilometres. This plain, a region of swampland where the water in many places is just an inch or two deep and the tall saw-grass grows, was called "Pahayokee", or river of grass by the Indians. In addition to alligators and crocodiles, over three hundred species of tropical birds and more than six hundred species of fish have been found here. Strict protection measures saved the alligators from becoming extinct here in the 1960s, and now there are once again around a million of these reptiles crawling through the swamps of Florida. The southern part of the Everglades provides a refuge for the North American crocodile. Visitors, however, rarely get to see this animal, which lives mainly in salt water. The wide variety of sights to be seen in this, the largest subtropical wilderness in the United States, have made the Everglades one of the most famous parks in the world. *11, 40*

FORT JEFFERSON ⑨. Like emeralds cast into the sea, a group of coral islands shimmers in the Gulf of Mexico seventy miles/one-hundred-ten kilometres to the west of Key West. The Spanish conquistador Juan Ponce de León gave the

Disney World. Top: Main Street, with Cinderella's Castle in the background.
Bottom: The Peking Temple of Heaven in Epcot Center.

islands the name "tortugas", after the turtles he found, and his sailors dubbed them "dry" because there was no fresh water to be found. On the largest island of the Dry Tortugas, a hexagonal fort was built, using German and Irish labour, in the hope that it would be of strategic importance. Fame came to Fort Jefferson in 1865 when four men were sentenced to a life of hard labour on the island. The four had played a major part in the plan to assassinate the then president, Abraham Lincoln. The fort can be visited by seaplane, or by boat, putting out from Key West.

FORT LAUDERDALE ⑩, the "Venice of Florida", is criss-crossed by a network of over 150 miles/250 kilometres of navigable canals. In the summer there are sailing regattas and fishing competitions, and all year round concerts and markets are held. Port Everglades, the modern harbour of Fort Lauderdale, not only plays an important role in freight shipping, it also provides anchorage for luxury liners destined for South America and the Caribbean. *30/31*

GATORLAND ZOO near Orlando ⑱ claims to be the largest alligator and

FLORIDA
CONCISE TRAVEL GUIDE

crocodile farm in the world. Over six thousand of the creatures splash around in its swamps; there are also snakes, tapirs, monkeys and birds to be seen. Experiments are in progress on the artificial insemination of crocodiles. You must not miss the animals' feeding time, when dangerous crocodiles and alligators hurl themselves into the air, competing for their share of the food. The jungle garden at Gatorland, where the ground is hidden by a dense carpet of ferns, was where some of the scenes in the second Indiana Jones film were shot. In the restaurant they serve alligator stew.

HOMOSASSA SPRINGS NATURE WORLD
⑪. Anyone who has never seen a

Jacksonville, financial centre of Florida.

Old booster rockets in the Rocket Garden at the Kennedy Space Center.

manatee will get their best chance to do so here. Nature World, north of Tampa on the west coast of Florida, is one of the last refuges of the manatee; here, too, injured and orphaned manatees are reared and protected. Manatees are strictly protected – there are only about 1,500 of them left in Florida. Since the females of these marine mammals only produce a single offspring every three to four years, it is uncertain whether the gentle giants will survive; every year around eighty manatees die as a result of accidents caused by man. In the crystal-clear springwaters of Homosassa Springs there also live more than forty species of fish, which can be watched from an underwater observation station.

INDIAN TEMPLE MOUND MUSEUM, a small building with exhibits demonstrating the prehistoric lives of the Indians of northern Florida, is in Fort Walton ⑫ on the west coast. Ceramic figures and other historically valuable pottery, shell jewellery, and a temple mound over seventy feet/twenty-one metres high clearly reveal Central American influences. The speculations of archaeologists that there is a connection between the ancient cultures of Mississippi and Mexico seem to have some justification.

JACKSONVILLE ⑬ is the largest city in Florida in population (586,000), the largest city in the United States in area (810 square miles/2,100 square kilometres – both figures from 1988), and the commercial and financial centre of the Sunshine State. With its important commercial port, steadily growing transport industry and banks, Jacksonville is becoming the rival of Atlanta, the other major commercial city in the south. In agreement with industrial sponsors and other backers, the city fathers decided in 1988 to have parts of the old town and the wooden riverbank promenade restored.

JAI ALAI is a ball game a little like tennis, in which a ball (*pelota*) is caught in a curved wicker basket (*cesta*) and thrown against a wall; the object of the game is to put the ball out of reach of the opponent. Originally a traditional Basque game, known in the Pyrenees as pelota, jai alai is the oldest and fastest ball game in the world. Ten of the fourteen courts, or *frontons*, in the United States are in Florida, and the best players come from the Spanish-speaking population.

KENNEDY SPACE CENTER/SPACEPORT USA ⑭. At the beginning of the 1950s Cape Canaveral was just a small research laboratory where engineers were trying to develop intercontinental rockets. After a great humiliation for the United States – the first man in space was not an American! – President John F. Kennedy called upon the country and its scientists to conquer the universe. Money being no object, the small laboratory was expanded into a space station, and research and rocket construction were greatly accelerated; as a result, on 20 July 1969, the astronaut Neil Armstrong was the first person to set foot on the moon. This event was greeted with rapture in the western world. Five more moon landings followed in the course of the next few years.

At the entrance to the Space Center is the Rocket Garden in which old booster rockets and space capsules are on display. The focal point for visitors at the Kennedy Space Center is called Spaceport; here the successes of the American space programme are celebrated in both film and some of the most amazing photographs from outer space.

FLORIDA
CONCISE TRAVEL GUIDE

KEY WEST ⑮. The name "Keys", like so many other names in Florida, derives from the Spanish. *Cayos* (little islands) became the American "Keys". US Highway 1 hops from island to island over forty-two bridges, connecting the mainland with the city of Key West over one hundred miles/one-hundred-seventy kilometres away.

A cheerful atmosphere pervades the town at the end of the road, where a permanent holiday mood, exotic and tropical, seems to prevail. As if by command, people pour into Mallory Square every evening to experience the sunset, which bathes everything in a red-gold light. Conjurers and jugglers perform their arts, a tightrope-walker balances with burning torches, and the spectators applaud when the red ball of fire sinks into the sea.

Many celebrities have come to the island over the last hundred years, among them President Harry S. Truman and writers and artists seeking peace and inspiration. Undoubtedly the most famous inhabitant of the island was Ernest Hemingway, who lived here for twelve years from 1928 onwards; one of the books he wrote during this time was *For Whom the Bell Tolls*. His well-maintained villa (Whitehead Street Nr. 907), with its tropical garden and innumerable cats, is open to visitors. Pulitzer Prize winner Tennessee Williams lived in Key West for thirty-four years, writing his plays *The Glass Menagerie* and *Cat on a Hot Tin Roof*. Key West is fascinating, glaringly commercial and at the same time delightfully quirky. In spite of all the changes it has undergone, the island has retained the exotic character which is its charm and continues to attract visitors. *14, 15*

KUDZU is an import from Asia. Once introduced as an ornamental plant to provide greenery in the garden, it escaped into the wild and now threatens to overrun the southern states.

LAKE OKEECHOBEE ⑯. In the language of the Seminole Indians, Okeechobee means big water; the lake is Florida's largest fresh-water reservoir. When in 1928 a hurricane (hurricanes in those days were not given names) whipped the water over its banks, destroying crops and claiming human lives,

President Herbert Hoover had dams built and irrigation channels laid out. Today, the land around Okeechobee is one of the most fertile vegetable and sugarcane growing areas. The lake and its waterways, which link it to the two coasts and the Everglades, were important routes of transport for the Seminole Indians, and also for the early settlers. There are large areas around Okeechobee which have not yet been developed for tourism, and which for that very reason are the private escapes for many Florida-lovers.

MGM-DISNEY FILM STUDIOS. These studios, like the Epcot Center, are part of the massive amusement zone of Orlando ⑱ and Disney World. Here, for the first time in the history of motion pictures, visitors are not only shown how television and cinema films are made, they also have the chance to spend the whole day behind or in front of the cameras, and participate in the making of real films.

MIAMI AND MIAMI BEACH ⑰. Here you will find everything that constitutes an American seaside resort: hotels, skyscrapers, wide roads, endless sandy beaches and inviting blue sea. The villas of the super-rich, hidden away in their lavish gardens, countless golf clubs and country clubs, and world-renowned

The Old Man and the Sea: the Keys.

The Art Deco quarter of Miami Beach has had protected status since 1979.

banks all create an ambiance of elegance and luxury.

Miami and Miami Beach are two distinct towns separated by Biscayne Bay, which is crossed by bridges carrying six-lane highways. Miami is the commercial and financial centre. Miami Beach is the seaside resort. In this "Latin American metropolis on North American soil", Cubans, Mexicans and immigrants from elsewhere in South America make up around fifty percent of the population (1988 figure). The Cubans, who left their homes after the Batista regime was toppled by Fidel Castro, have played a considerable part in the commercial

FLORIDA
CONCISE TRAVEL GUIDE

The old fortress at St. Augustine, the oldest settlement in North America.

revitalisation of the city. When you enter "Little Havana", it feels as if you have left Miami behind. The heart of this Cuban enclave is 8th Street Southwest, locally known as "Calle Ocho". Here, hot dogs are called *perros calientes*, and every café serves Café Cubano, strong coffee which is drunk from tiny little cups. In "Little Havana", English is a foreign language. *2, 17, 21, 23, 35, 44/45, 46*

NATIONAL KEY DEER REFUGE. In this nature reserve not far from Key West ⑮, conservationists and rangers are trying to save the last remaining white-tailed Key Deer. These dainty little animals, barely waist high, with their white rump patches and short tails, can be seen in the morning and late afternoon at the roadside. A fine of up to 1,000 dollars is imposed on anyone caught by the rangers feeding these endangered animals.

ORLANDO ⑱ is the fastest growing city in the United States. The city authorities are way behind with their numbering and naming because so many new buildings and roads spring up every week. Orlando was once a small farming community with a trading post where the soldiers who had fought the Seminoles hung around. When the first "iron horse" reached Orlando in 1880, orange and lemon pickers came and settled, and a small town grew up, although it still did not attract much attention. In the 1950s Orlando started to get an influx of people from the north who liked the mild climate and wanted to relax in the quiet of the countryside and lakes. In 1963–64, however, the men from the Walt Disney Company came and began buying up swampland southwest of Orlando. Within no time at all, nearly forty-five square miles/one-hundred-fifteen square kilometres were in the possession of the cartoon maker – and the peace was gone for ever. From that point on, the mouse from Hollywood was on the advance.

PALM BEACH ⑲. Henry Flagler and his railway played an important part in the settlement of the east coast of Florida. So it was with Palm Beach. When the line reached this part of the coast in 1894, the railway magnate had his sumptuous Grand Hotel built there, which soon became frequented by the rich. When he was planning his own house, he commissioned the architects who had designed the Metropolitan Opera House in New York. It was built in 1901 at a cost of two and a half million dollars. Today, the lavishly appointed house is a museum. Palm Beach has remained a mecca for the rich, although with the coming of mass tourism it has lost something of its exclusivity.

THE PANHANDLE is the name by which northern Florida is known. If you look at the state boundary of Florida you will notice a kind of handle or shaft which attaches the peninsula to the mainland.

QUIET WATERS PARK. When the hustle and bustle in Fort Lauderdale ⑩ simply becomes too much for the locals, they take themselves away to this park. The lake really is quiet – motor boats are prohibited. Only fishing, rowing and sailing are permitted.

RINGLING MUSEUM OF ART. John Ringling called his circus performances "The Greatest Show on Earth"; his museum is also held to be an important cultural asset. John Ringling (1866–1936), director of the Ringling Brothers and Barnum & Bailey circus empire, had amassed a fabulous fortune and in the 1920s he invested it in oil wells, railways, property, and above all, art. He chose Sarasota ⑳, a town south of Tampa, as the winter home for his circus, and there he built a mansion and a Florentine villa with exhibition rooms. In his search for exciting circus acts, he and his wife Mable frequently travelled in Europe where he began collecting old masterpieces. While the baroque style, in particular, attracted him with its elaborate embellishments and flourishes, he was a tireless collector of Greek and Roman statues. Works by Rubens, Rembrandt and El Greco and 750 baroque paintings can be viewed in the large exhibition halls. There are also other rooms dedicated to modern painting and photography. The Ringlings' passion for collecting things even went as far as entire buildings, as illustrated by the Asolo Theatre: the complete interior of a Venetian theatre dating from the eighteenth century, which they had dismantled and shipped to Florida.

SEA WORLD, Sea World Drive, Orlando ⑱ boasts a large pool where the famous killer whale Shamu is presented to the public every day. Through meticulous training he and other sea animals have been taught to give astonishing performances, which have helped to make Sea World famous around the world. In the neighbouring buildings live sea lions, otters, dolphins, a walrus and over one hundred penguins. *34*

ST. AUGUSTINE ㉑, on the northern coast of Florida, the oldest town in America,

FLORIDA
CONCISE TRAVEL GUIDE

is Florida's historic treasure house. Here, everything bears the prefix "the oldest": the schoolhouse, the shop, the Spanish Quarter, and even what is believed to be the oldest house in America. The cathedral of St. Augustine, built in 1797, is naturally the home of the oldest parish in America. A visit to the Spanish Quarter gives a good impression of life in days gone by; you feel transported back 250 years in time. In a dozen faithfully restored buildings from early colonial times, "residents" dressed in period costume act out the simple lives of the soldiers and families of those days most convincingly. At the harbour in the Old Town of St. Augustine, it is possible to visit the Castillo de San Marcos. From its fortifications there is a lovely view over the harbour and the town.

ST. PETERSBURG ㉒ was founded by Peter Demens, a Russian aristocrat from the time of the czars. In 1888 he reached the Gulf of Mexico with his Orange Belt Railroad, which he ran straight across Florida from the Atlantic coast. The last station on the line he proudly named after his hometown, Saint Petersburg.
In the harbour lies The Bounty, the ship made famous by the film Mutiny on the Bounty. More famous still, however, is the Dalí Museum in downtown St. Petersburg. The building with Dalí's signature above the entrance houses the world's largest collection of the surrealist's pictures: ninety-five oil paintings, over two hundred drawings, watercolours and lithographs, and more than one thousand sculptures, prints and films. A complete tour of the museum shows how the work of this artistic genius developed.

TALLAHASSEE ㉓ (meaning old fields in the language of the Creek Indians) is the capital of Florida, but fortunately, with a population in 1988 of about 90,000, it has never made the leap to big city status. Florida's population and industry have shifted southwards while the administration has remained here. The only tall building in the town is the Capitol, a clumsy structure which looks really out of place in this small town. Tallahassee, among other things, is the home of the Florida State Archives, the ground floor of which houses the excellent Historical Museum. *33, 37*

The Pier in St. Petersburg.

The Vietnam Memorial in Florida's reserved capital city Tallahassee.

TAMPA ㉔ (approximately 300,000 residents) is situated at the eastern end of the Howard Frankland Bridge spanning Tampa Bay and linking St. Petersburg with Tampa. On the northern outskirts of downtown Tampa lies Ybor City, the historical Latin Quarter, where in 1920 ten thousand cigar-rollers were turning out 300 million cigars per year. The cigar workers resisted the introduction of tobacco processing machines by taking industrial action, but without success. Almost all of them lost their jobs and moved away. Nevertheless, Tampa has remained the "cigar capital" of the USA: now three million cigars are rolled per day (1988 figures) – but by machine, not by hand.

TARPON SPRINGS. Twenty-five miles/forty kilometres north of St. Petersburg ㉒ you would think you were no longer in Florida. What you see is a Greek village, its main street lined with white-washed houses and colourful shops, with the aroma of garlic wafting from its tavernas. Down in the harbour boats are unloaded, and here and there snatches of Greek songs can be heard from the houses. Fifty years ago, Tarpon Springs was the "sponge capital" of the world, where skillful Greek divers brought up sponges from the sea bed. The sponge trade blossomed and thousands of Greek emigrants made a living from it, until a virus wiped out virtually the entire sponge population around the Gulf coast. The Greeks and their village remained. In the side streets you will find little Greek Orthodox churches, and from the bakeries drifts the smell of freshly-baked almond cakes. *25*

USEPPA ISLAND. This island, not far from Fort Myers ㉕, has gone down in history because it was here that the Spanish pirate José Gaspar imprisoned his sweethearts. One of these women, the young Joseffa, refused him, so he had her beheaded on the spot. The very name of

FLORIDA
CONCISE TRAVEL GUIDE

Sponges on sale in Tarpon Springs, former sponge capital of the world.

the island arose from the legends and stories surrounding Joseffa and the pirates: Joseffa became Useppa. Today the island is privately owned, and the stylish holiday village is open only to club members; non-members are welcome only if they book a minimum seven day holiday.

VILLA VIZCAYA MUSEUM AND GARDENS near Miami ⑰ is an experience not to be missed. This is where the American industrial tycoon James Deering created his winter residence in the year 1916. The sumptuous mansion was designed on the European model, and was filled with art treasures and furniture from all over the world. Over the two years it took to build the villa, more than one thousand men worked on it at various different times. Half of the seventy rooms are open to the public. The garden, with its exotic plants, pools, wells and statues, is just like the gardens of the Italian palazzi. There is even a garden for the blind, with strongly aromatic herbs and flowers, and sculptures to feel.

WAKULLA SPRINGS, near Tallahassee ㉓, is the name of a spring nearly two hundred feet/sixty metres deep and a few hundred yards in diameter, which is the source of the river of the same name. Thoroughly filtered and purified through the limestone rock, the water is forced under pressure to the surface. You can take a trip in a glass-bottomed boat to see the fish, crawfish and alligators swimming in the crystal-clear water. Wakulla Springs is a protected nature reserve. As well as ancient cypress trees, there are also green and shimmering glossy ibises, pink spoonbills, egrets and other birds to be seen. *38/39, 43*

WEEKI WACHEE SPRINGS ㉖. In the limpid waters of Weeki Wachee Springs, about sixty miles/one hundred kilometres north of St. Petersburg, "mermaids" put on an impressive underwater show. An excursion in a glass-bottomed boat also takes you past the Pelican Orphanage.

XANADU. For some time now, the twenty-first century has already been a reality in this fully electronic house near Orlando ⑱. Visitors can order meals from a computer screen and the food is then cooked automatically. Individual meals can be made up from a menu of some five hundred items, and the calorie, cholesterol and fat content, together with other data, are calculated. The house was built on energy-saving lines, and no harmful building materials were used in its construction. Waste is recycled, and the house runs on solar energy and energy derived from waste materials.

YULEE SUGAR MILL RUINS HISTORIC SITE near Crystal River ㉗, 125 miles/200 kilometres north of St. Petersburg, is a partially restored sugar mill which once belonged to Senator David Yulee. During the American Civil War, Yulee supplied the Confederates with sugar products until Union troops burned this sugar mill down.

LIST OF SOURCES AND ILLUSTRATIONS

Thomas Barbour, *That Vanishing Eden. A Naturalist's Florida.* Boston: Little, Brown & Co., 1945.

William Bartram, *Travels through North and South Carolina, Georgia, East and West Florida.* Philadelphia: 1791.

Alistair Cooke, *One Man's America.* New York: Alfred A. Knopf, 1953.

Marjory Stoneman Douglas, *Florida: The Long Frontier.* New York: Harper & Row, 1967.

Ernest Hemingway, *To Have and Have Not.* London: Grafton Books, 1972.

David Rieff, *Going to Miami.* New York: Penguin Books Ltd., 1987.

Harriet Beecher Stowe, "The Labourers of the South," in *Palmetto Leaves.* Boston: J.R. Osgood & Co., 1873.

We would like to thank all copyright holders and publishers for their kind permission to reprint. In a few cases, we were not able to find out who the copyright holders are, despite having made intensive efforts to do so. Those to whom this applies are asked to contact us.

The map on page 48 was supplied by Astrid Fischer, Munich and is reprinted with the kind permission of Polyglott Verlag, Munich.

All other photographs were supplied by Udo Bernhart.

DESTINATION FLORIDA
WINDSOR BOOKS INTERNATIONAL, 1992

© 1990 by Verlag C.J. Bucher GmbH
Munich and Berlin
Translation: Jane Parry
Editor: Karen Lemiski
Anthology: Carmel Finnan, Karen Lemiski

All rights reserved
Printed and bound in Germany
ISBN 1 874111 02 2